LIBRARY OC

D0396166

Ready to Launch
THE PR COUTURE GUIDE TO BREAKING INTO FASHION PR
BY CROSBY NORICKS

LIBRARY OC

DEMCO

Cover Image: Lindsay Garvey
Cover Design: Queen City Studio
Copyright © 2011 Crosby Noricks
All rights reserved.
ISBN: 978-1467939973
Visit prcouture.com for more information

Tell me, what is it you
plan to do with your one
wild and precious life?

– Mary Oliver

CONTENTS

INTRODUCTION

Hi. You look very nice today.

Thank you so much for spending some hard-earned could be used for fashion cash on *Ready to Launch: The PR Couture Guide to Breaking into Fashion PR*. The idea for this book has been rattling around in my head for years. I am, as they say in every press release, thrilled to be sharing my knowledge and experience, combined with the expertise and advice of close to thirty other fashion PR pros, with you in this format. With this guide you now have insider knowledge specific to working in fashion public relations including, what to expect from a career in fashion PR, job interview questions, social media networking tactics and contact information for some of the top fashion PR agencies. And that's just the beginning!

One of my favorite things about running PR Couture is the opportunity it affords me to connect with, learn from and then share the experiences and stories of fashion PR professionals with my readers. That's why this guide is filled with not only my own experience, but also first-hand accounts of career growth, transition and tips from agency CEOs to interns. We all have to start somewhere and we can all learn from each other!

To begin, I wanted to spend a bit of time taking you through my own "breaking in" story. After amassing close to a decade of professional (and personal!) experience working in fashion PR and consumer marketing, for agencies, in-house and for myself, I have the decided advantage of being able to look back and, as Steve Jobs explained to students at Stanford University during his commencement speech, "connect the dots."

> *You can't connect the dots looking forward; you can only connect them looking backwards. So you have to trust that the dots will somehow connect in your future. You have to trust in something — your gut, destiny, life, karma, whatever.*
>
> *- Steve Jobs (Forbes.com)*

So, settle in and let's begin!

My Story

I wasn't born into the fashion industry. However, I did have a dress up box filled with my mom's finds from vintage shops, estate sales, thrift stores and swap meets from the time I could walk. It was my favorite "toy." My grandmother dabbled in estate sales for prominent families in Santa Barbara, and my mother was a stylish artist turned Spanish teacher who spent the seventies making many of her clothes by hand, despite being adamant about hating to sew.

From a very early age, clothing was about play, make-believe, dressing up and exploration. While other kids were, I don't know, playing soccer or camping, I was spending afternoons cutting out different looks from teen fashion magazines that I then collaged into a binder. On weekends, I tried to get pieces from my closet to match what I saw in the magazines and, as a girl forced to wear a uniform to school until fifth grade, waited eagerly for "free dress" days where I could show off my latest creations. As I grew older, my family moved several times, and I daydreamed about becoming a stylist, a buyer, or maybe the owner of my own boutique. On long car rides I would sketch out logos and make notes in my journal. I continued to obsess over fashion magazines, Anthropologie catalogs, and (this is the part where I date myself), shows like *House of Style* on MTV. In high school I escaped to San Francisco and Berkeley to people watch and shop vintage and consignment shops. I took inspiration from

Liv Tyler's character in *Stealing Beauty*, Milla Jovovich's romantic dresses and bobbed hair, Courtney Love's slips and fishnets and Frida Kahlo's bright colors and nod to the masculine silhouette. My favorite looks were romantic, vintage dresses or 1970s novelty tees, mixed in with finds from the Army Surplus store - wide-legged wool US Navy pants (so many buttons!) and structured olive green Army jackets. Of course, I might be looking at this with rose-tinted glasses and glossing over some fashion trends I would rather forget, like bodysuits, oversized flannels and the year I wore skate shoes to homecoming. Yes, that happened.

And so, while I was known for having "good style," (whatever that means!), and a killer eye when it came to thrift store shopping, I had no idea how the actual fashion industry worked or how one set about becoming a part of it. Instead, I had three out of four parents immersed in independent schools, and another that sold sugar and arrived home with chocolate bars rather than couture. I knew I wanted to work in fashion but I didn't know how or where or in what capacity.

I started with art and travel. I took painting classes at the Academy of Art in San Francisco, spent summers in Mexico and Ecuador exploring, shopping, and getting to know myself, still sure that I wanted to, somehow, work in fashion. But HOW?!

I turned seventeen and spent the summer living it up in the (college!) dorms with other creative types at a summer program at the California Academy of the Arts in Oakland. There I learned I was hopeless at fashion illustration and draping (muslin and I are not friends), but enjoyed painting. Most importantly, I was introduced to art kids, punk music and its corresponding fashion, the likes of which rarely made it out to the San Francisco suburb where I was stationed at the time. Being immersed in the land of sketch pads and crafty nights spent turning men's underwear into halter tops (yes, there are pictures – eep!), cemented my desire to find a job that would allow me to both be creative and to work with other creative people.

A serious dose of misguided romantic antics (don't we all have a few of those), coupled with a big yucky fear that I didn't look right (read: wasn't thin/pretty enough) or have the right connections/confidence to play the part of aspiring fashion editor in New York City meant that I only applied to college in California. I went to the one that offered me the most scholarship money but no classes in fashion, advertising, marketing, nada. What they did offer was a media studies major, so I studied films - documentaries, art films, blockbusters - and snuck in some web design and animation classes. In the spring of my junior year, I packed my bags (two bulging, oversized rolling suitcases = awkward maneuvering through Heathrow and cobbled streets) for a semester studying abroad at the

London College of Fashion, with visions of twenty-something Vivienne Westwood's dancing in my head.

Alas, as part of a sequestered United States-only study abroad group made up of mostly retail majors, we took classes on our own track, with limited to no contact with the students attending the college. This was a bit of a letdown. However, two important things happened. First, I realized that my liberal-arts education and exploration of feminist studies had given me a rather unique point of view when it came to exploring fashion as an industry. While I was connecting fashion to things like cultural and subculture identity, sexual politics, feminism and art, my fellow students were marveling at the gorgeous dress in the latest Prada print ad and all wore identical black pants. The second thing was that I took a class in fashion PR. Although much of the work was rather, uhm, shallow, an exercise where we had to take inspiration from a fashion photograph to create a product, name, and launch party concept had me over the moon and was my favorite exercise of the semester (and one I have since replicated with students).

I arrived home from London with a pair of beloved green velvet pants picked up at a fashion student trunk sale, a lip ring, and an idea for an undergraduate thesis that would explore the relationship between the fashion industry and the feminist movement, from early 20th century to present day. I wrote an undergraduate thesis and hosted a fashion/ art installation where people could create their own interpretation of feminist fashion. There was a lot of tulle and spray paint involved!
Now comes the part in the movie with the montage of girl-turned-woman getting her career together, except in reality it was slow, often painful and took several years. I dyed my hair pink, red and pink again, graduated from college and moved to Los Angeles where I went on too many embarrassing, awful interviews to count.

My first job out of college was at the Buffalo Exchange in Hollywood, which, while not a job doing wardrobe for film or working at a production studio like I wanted, did pay above minimum wage. It also provided ample time to rummage through clothes all day long and learn labels at the hands of the stylists and designers who often dropped off their photo shoot discards and samples. I spent several months in Barcelona where I took hip-hop dance classes daily, nursed a broken heart and made friends with the sales associates at Zara. With no money or job, I moved back home. Oh the horror.

I spent a year working the front desk and helping plan special events for an upscale full-service salon, with generally no idea what I was doing. So I decided to go back to school. Just before my 24th birthday, I moved to San Diego and within two weeks had a job working in fashion PR. I also started graduate school. Funny how things can go so slowly for so long and then speed up.

While pursuing my master's degree in Communication I learned about advertising, public relations and communication theory. During my first year, I realized that the program was highly theoretical and lacking in practical application. I wanted to create campaigns, not read about them! Eventually I connected again to fashion and that PR class in London. I liked the idea that while advertising was pay for play, PR required more skill, at least in my estimation! I began to think about the idea of PR in the fashion industry and took a few classes in public relations and one in event and venue management, all of which were more hands-on than my other classes.

When it came time to write my graduate thesis, my advisor encouraged me to explore fashion PR as a thesis topic. And so, this girl began to explore a theory of fashion PR, looking at traditional PR theory, feminist PR theory, dress studies and fashion marketing.

I searched online and offline looking for literature that touched on the communication functions within the fashion industry. Finding little, I began to take bits and pieces from what I did find, in order to develop a PR theory specific to fashion. I also went straight to the source and completed a series of in-depth interviews with fashion PR practitioners. While LA was manageable, New York was a different story! I won't take you through the small town girl in the big city experience of doormen, model casting calls, cabs and not always so welcoming (though some were incredibly warm and wonderful) interviews, but it was quite the experience! All in all, interviewing those "PR girls" was the very best thing I could have done, both for my research, as well as my career. These women were smart, driven, and of course, well dressed! They opened my eyes to the realities, challenges and perks of the job.

During graduate school I worked thirty hours a week managing the PR and marketing department for a jewelry company based in San Diego that specialized in getting the "Celebrity Look for Less." In this position, I worked directly with fashion editors on a daily basis to pull product that was then photographed and placed in glossy magazines, after which we all did a happy dance. I also designed and managed several weekly marketing emails, helped to design the first print catalog, and eventually managed a team.

After two years working in-house, I was curious to experience what it would be like working at a PR agency. I had become friends with a woman in my graduate program who was the director at a local PR agency. Toward the end of school I began to work for her to help grow and sustain the burgeoning lifestyle division (fashion, food, interior design), at that agency.

I had experienced frustration at how little information was available about fashion PR during my thesis research. One weekend I decided to create a blog to be able to continue my connection to the work I had done and to begin to share a bit about what I learned. I created PR Couture over the course of a few days, and slowly began to write and connect with others in the field.

On the career side, I was working a lot with fashion, celebrity, mom and eco—fashion bloggers and really enjoyed the experience of both being a blogger and working with them on behalf of clients. Over the next several years I worked at several different agencies as well as for myself, on everything from the launch of a fashion boutique to helping to organize and promote a citywide sleep-out to raise money and awareness for a local homeless shelter. Meanwhile, in my spare (ha!) time I wrote articles for PR Couture, connected with other fashion bloggers and brands, and interviewed other fashion PR practitioners, grilling them on their life and approach to the work.

Some personal career highlights followed over the next few years, including being sponsored by Microsoft to attend New York Fashion Week and being one of the first bloggers invited by WWDMagic and *Teen Vogue* to cover the tradeshow. I taught fashion communication courses at FIDM and the Art Institute. In San Diego I was named "Blogger of the Year," and the next year *944 Magazine* did a feature on me (photo shoot included!). PR Couture became the gateway to finding my own little corner of the fashion PR world.

PR Couture also helped me to transition out of traditional PR. In 2008 I had the opportunity to spearhead the social media department for an award-winning agency in San Diego, and I took it! These days I help all sorts of brands develop and execute social media strategies that connect companies to customers to build long—term loyalty and rapport. Occasionally, I get to work in collaboration with a brand's existing PR agency, which I did recently for a beauty brand during Fashion Week. It's always fun to bring my PR experience to the table and work with and understand the multiple goals and perspectives driving a campaign.

Most recently. I have begun to offer one-on-one consulting with students and entry-level practitioners as well as fashion PR agency owners and brands. I've discovered that what I really love to do is very similar is to what I discovered back at art school at seventeen; I enjoy using my skills to help brands and people I admire to be able to make a living doing what they love, whether it's a future fashion PR pro, fashion brand or something completely different.

This is a very long-winded story to make the point that fashion exists everywhere, fashion is personal, and with initiative and steadfastness, you can break in wherever and whenever you please. It just might not be the way that you think.

As PR Couture celebrates her fifth birthday, it seems only fitting that the girl who began PR Couture in order to find out more about the profession is now writing a book about how to get started. I want to thank you, from the bottom of my dress-up girl heart, for your support of PR Couture and your support of you, for taking the risks you take every day, to make the choices that will eventually allow you to connect the dots.

In love and petticoats,

Crosby

Resources and Links
There are a ton of great resources listed in this book. For easy clicking, please visit http://prcouture.com/readytolaunch and enter password "Success." This will take you to a secret page of links. It will also be updated quarterly to help ensure the information included in here is up-to-date. And please, keep the password to yourself!

BASICS

What is PR and how is it different from marketing or advertising?

Pick up any PR textbook and you will likely encounter a definition of public relations that describes it as the management function. This is just a fancy way of ensuring that PR gets to play at the big kid table – with other top-level executives. It will say something about PR being responsible for the communication between an organization (brand, company) and it's publics (customers, neighbors, partners, board members), and that the goal of PR is to ensure a mutually beneficial relationship, i.e. both the organization and public get something of value out of the exchange.

> *Today's PR professional understands the intersection of content, social technologies and marketing in ways that achieve common PR objectives: credibility, thought leadership and influence. It's less about managing information flow and pushing content – and more about creating content, networking and engagement.*
>
> *- Lee Odden, Top Rank Marketing (Heidicohen.com)*

In practice however, public relations varies wildly, in different industries as well as from agency to agency. Additionally, PR has had to evolve rapidly in the past several years as the result of mass adoption of online communication channels (Facebook, Twitter) and the explosion of online media (magazines, blogs). These new communication tools have led to crossover into other communication disciplines (advertising, marketing, customer service).

With the lines blurring, it can be helpful to clarify what PR is, by first examining what it is not.

Marketing

Outside of PR pitching to land media coverage, the difference between marketing and PR can be a bit nebulous. Both require strategic planning and a series of tactics, both are concerned with helping to achieve business goals, both focus on the brand image and unique selling point (marketing) or key messages (PR). In fact, there is a longstanding debate about whether or not PR (along with advertising) is a part of the "marketing mix" (traditionally price, product, place, and promotion) or should be treated as its own separate, and not always equal, department. The answer to that often depends on if you are asking a publicist or a marketer!

If public relations is concerned with driving awareness, building brand reputation and "the story," marketing is more explicitly concerned with "the sale" and the bottom line. The messaging may be similar, and of course sales are a component of PR, but the marketing department is most often concerned with tactics to drive immediate purchases like email marketing, coupons and incentives. Traditionally, PR tactics focused on gaining media attention, while marketing focused more on customer sales. However, social media has changed the playing field a bit, and PR is now concerned with more than just media and may be more involved in customer relationship building.

Advertising

The difference between advertising and PR is pretty straightforward. Essentially, advertising is paid media, meaning that companies purchase ad space in a magazine, blog or billboard and then put the ad they have concepted, created and finalized into the space they paid for. By paying for space, the company has total creative and message control over what is placed. In PR, you are typically working with an editor or journalist and are at the mercy of what they print!

The media relations function of public relations, the part where we pitch the media to cover clients in a newspaper, morning show, magazine, etc. is instead considered earned media. A PR professional or company doesn't purchase a front-page story in *The New York Times*, instead they encourage the reporter, editor or news producer that the company or product has enough value or relevancy to merit coverage. Because the resulting story is not an advertisement, PR doesn't have ultimate control over what or how the story is written or the product is portrayed. However, because the consumer knows that companies pay for advertisement and can put whatever they want there, the idea is that PR carries more credibility. For example, when flipping through *Lucky Magazine*, a full-page advertisement for DVF may have less impact on a potential customer than a fashion editor listing the dress as her "fall must-have." The idea here is that the editor, being seen as a fashionable, industry expert, has a greater influence on the magazine reader. As a result, her third-party endorsement of the dress is more meaningful than a paid advertisement for the dress.

Because media coverage is never guaranteed, PR is often tasked to justify its value against advertising or marketing. Additionally, the difference between earned and paid media (advertising) leads many companies to prefer to place money on a "sure thing," despite the fact that public relations often comes at a lower cost than traditional advertising. However, while public relations can often be less expensive overall than the cost of setting up a photo or video shoot, designing or editing the ad, and then paying thousands, sometimes hundreds of thousands of dollars for placement, time is still money.

The time and skill it takes the PR professional to first develop relationships with media, then create a pitch that is customized to the needs of each individual media professional, and then to be able to craft multiple angles and opportunities to ensure ongoing coverage on behalf of clients is work! It requires creativity, strategy and an investment of time and resources.

Public Relations

In summary, public relations often focuses primarily on securing media (press) coverage for clients. However, PR is also the communication function responsible for nurturing the relationship between a company and well, anybody who is interested. For practitioners, this may mean interfacing directly with customers, or shareholders, performing crisis communication (the actions a company takes when something has gone wrong), and community outreach, in addition to working with the media.

FASHION PR

So, what does a fashion publicist do?

When learning about public relations in school, textbooks and academic journals typically focus on big business industries like healthcare, technology or automotive. So-called "softer" industries like lifestyle, entertainment, fashion and beauty are seen as less strategic and even less credible among the PR elite. As such, they rarely get any class-time, despite the fact that many PR students are interested in working in the industries listed above. One of the things I explored in my thesis was the idea of strategic fashion public relations – which I found to be explicitly the case among the majority of practitioners I interviewed. However, fashion PR does often place a primary focus on securing product-based editorial coverage as well as events (trunk shows, runway shows, tradeshows), so it can be bit more media-heavy that other types of PR.

The Betsey Johnson PR department has their hands in every project and works to support every single department.

– Brianna Saperstein, PR Intern, Betsey Johnson

While it varies depending on the size of the company, a fashion publicist is often explicitly involved in the overall brand direction, and therefore might consult and offer expertise on everything from creative concepts for an upcoming photo shoot to working with marketing to promote an exclusive preview of a new collection via Facebook. Typical daily work may include media kits, press releases and pitches, pitching traditional (print magazines, television, newspapers) and digital (online publications, bloggers) media, planning, hosting or attending events like trunk and fashion shows, responding to media requests, and managing social media accounts.

Traditionally fashion PR focused efforts focused on a primary goal of securing press placements in targeted media outlets to create and reinforce brand image. While this goal still exists, the methodology, variety and speed of securing "hits" has changed drastically.

There are many more outlets for PR today and with these options comes the responsibility to execute campaigns on a wider scale at an almost instantaneous pace. Today a fully flushed-out PR campaign needs to include electronic and digital outlets in addition to print. Social media strategy is crucial, as well as event planning/execution and a celebrity seeding program.

- Kristen Steinhilber Calavas, Director, Fashion Commerce Partnerships Sugar, Inc. President of TheLookbook.com

Fashion public relations is fast-paced, exciting and full of surprises – no two days are rarely alike, and the opportunity to work with fashion designers, stylists, vendors and media can be endlessly inspiring and motivating. However, the job is not one big party. It requires quick-thinking, confidence, multi-tasking, organizational skills, as well as the ability to communicate complex ideas quickly. The ability to develop almost instant rapport with strangers, manage egos and be one-step ahead of client needs and demands is required, as are incredible writing skills, an eye for detail and the ability to spot emerging trends.

I usually spend my days pitching magazines like Seventeen, Teen Vogue, Self, Lucky & People Style watch to get product placed in editorial stories. I also keep up with celeb stylists to find out what their needs are and send them items to try and get product placed with celebs.

I spend a lot of my days researching trends and pop culture to find innovative ways to highlight our product on our social media pages. I also spearhead major promotional events and cause marketing initiatives and coordinate them from corporate to our field teams. I also spend a lot of time checking emails, talking on the phone, updating media and writing press releases.

- Jennifer Lezan, PR & Social Media Coordinator, Claire's Inc.

In fashion PR, celebrity outreach is also a key component, as well as product placement, so a fashion publicist may also be working with celebrity stylists to pull clothing for an upcoming special event or award show.

Celebs typically have at least one personal assistant, manager, publicist, agent and style teams for wardrobe, hair and makeup. I constantly reach out to stylists and publicists on behalf of the designers, manufacturers and retailers we represent.

- Jen Cullen Wilson, Senior Account Executive, Luxury Brand Group

As a fashion PR professional, you typically have three options when it comes to working in the industry. You can work on multiple client accounts for a fashion PR agency like People's Revolution, in-house for a single brand like Aliza Licht (DKNY) or work as a freelance fashion PR practitioner, also known as being an independent contractor. There is also the opportunity to work at a showroom, helping buyers and stylists. Some fashion PR agencies have their own showrooms, but many are their own entities, and some, like Bel Esprit, are completely online.

In-House Fashion PR

Working in-house has a few distinct advantages, mainly that you are more integrated member of the team and have access to all the news, updates and goings-on, which is helpful when coming up with new ideas and identifying PR opportunities. However, for some of us, working on a single brand can become monotonous. Plus, working within a single company means missing out on the opportunity to learn from the successes (and failures) of multiple brands, which can provide great perspective, particularly when just starting out.

> *All operations regarding name, the brand, press, image, magazine credits, you name it- all goes through me. It's my job to make sure our company's image is presented in the best way possible. Fashion is a big world and it can be hard to control.*
>
> *You do spend time putting out fires, but mostly I spend my days focusing on gaining exposure for our line, whether is communicating with editors and seeing what styles they need for upcoming shoots, talking to celeb stylists and coordinating which looks would be great for their clients, setting up photo shoots and interviews and generally handling all business Jill Stuart related.*
>
> *- Lindsey Green, Director of Communications for Jill Stuart (TheGloss.com)*

During graduate school, I worked in-house for an e-commerce jewelry company that did a ton of work with all your favorite gossip mags. Seriously, ask me anything celebrity-gossip related between the years 2004-2006, after that...not so much! In that position I worked directly with the CEO, assisting with everything from PR strategy, brand development, advertising and marketing, to developing processes to improve internal and customer communications. I became an expert in this single brand, and much of the work I did was about solidifying existing media relationships and growing new ones. My challenges with working in-house included staying excited and challenged by work that eventually became routine, as well wearing about 100 hats with very little support.

Fashion PR Agency

Working for a PR agency is a great way to gain exposure into multiple brands, and because each one has its own specializations and personality, agency life also teaches you about what you like and don't like. At a smaller boutique agency, you might find that you really enjoy working so closely with emerging designers on their overall brand, or you may find that the big name brands with their clear brand guidelines and established name are more your style.

> *Public relations is a very fast-paced and deadline-driven environment. In order to be successful and produce results, you must always be one, if not two or three steps ahead. It is all about making things happen rather than waiting for them to occur, and exceeding the expectations. A good publicist is always working, even outside of the office. You're constantly looking for ways to promote and expand your brands and clients.*
>
> *- Shonte Shannon, PR Intern, Chic Little Devil PR*

Working on multiple accounts also teaches time (and client!) management, challenges creativity and ideation, and importantly, sheds light into the many different ways that companies are built, how they run, and what they value. It's not always pretty, but it's always enlightening!

As an account executive, I worked on multiple clients at a time. The variety in daily work was challenging and exciting, and meant that I might be reaching out to fashion blogs one day, and the next day stuffing gift bags for a trunk show at W Hotel. While I was no longer designing email newsletters or writing product copy for celebrity engagement rings, I did develop an entire PR launch plan for a new upscale boutique, coordinated a photo shoot with a local boutique hotel, wrote pitches, press releases, bios, sponsorship packages and website copy. Within the agency, the major pressure was to land publicity for our lifestyle clients. Unlike my past experience of coming into work with an inbox full of magazine requests, it was now my job to proactively make these editors interested in my clients' products. I learned quickly how difficult, but ultimately rewarding public relations could be. I also learned importance of treating the agency as its own client, which helped me later on when I struck out on my own.

Freelance Fashion Publicist

Some publicists prefer to work on their own as a one-woman (or man!) show, perhaps contracting with a few agencies on a project-by-project basis. A freelance publicist might specialize and be known for expertise in a particular aspect of PR. Perhaps she has strong international media contacts or he is well known among the local philanthropic set. While the freelance route can be great for an established name within the industry (along with strong media relationships and an air-tight reputation of course!), the freelance route can be challenging for those just starting out.

After being employed by a midsize apparel and accessories brand for a few years in NYC, I desperately craved change. Doing contract work for various other companies and brands prior to, and during that time was far more satisfying and challenging than my full time day-to-day. These days, I contract with clients in order to have more flexibility, control, and a greater sense of synergy with a multitude of clients. I also get to wear many different hats ranging from social media strategy, PR, web/e-commerce consulting, SEO and beyond.

Working freelance has its difficulties. Clients can be unpredictable; contracts can be held up or put on hold, which can lead to having an inconsistent schedule, as well as income flow. Additionally, you become responsible for drafting and enforcing contracts, purchasing your own insurance, paying that dreaded self-employment tax, and of course a thousand other things that might come up. I've learned to always expect the unexpected.

For me, the benefits of being strictly freelance far outweigh any drawbacks. Being on my own, with the occasional help from an assistant, allows me the flexibility to work from virtually anywhere in the world, with the clients I really want to work with, including the smaller brands, start-ups, and companies that simply don't have the budget or resources to hire an agency or someone in-house.

The majority of my clients come by way of referrals from current or previous partners, various firms who I've become strategically aligned with, or simply by word of mouth. Networking and having a broad skill-set are absolutely key to freelance success. Finally, if you can't "do it all" for a client, make sure you have someone to bring in on a project to do the things you cannot.

Deciding to go the freelance route can be a risky decision for anyone. But who gets anywhere in life without taking risks?

-Jennifer Bambrough, JDVB Media

For example, I had worked at a PR agency for just over a year when the three partners, let's call them A, B and C announced they were breaking up. A and B were staying together to start a new agency, and C was going to start his own agency. I was offered my same position and salary with A and B and the opportunity to freelance with C. The problem for me was that my favorite clients were being split up, and I didn't want to have to choose between them. Instead, I negotiated to work as an independent contractor for both, a decision that threw me into the deep end as I scrambled to adjust to the freelance life. Ultimately I figured out not only how to excel in PR but how to start a business.

As an independent contractor, you forgo the security of a steady paycheck, health insurance, and paying taxes just once a year for the freedom to set your own hours, work with the clients you want to work with, execute the PR strategy you believe will be most effective and be paid your full bill rate. While it can appear quite lucrative at first to be paid a full $100 an hour, rather than an annual salary that is less than half what your agency actually charges for your services, remember that those pesky estimated taxes you must now pay quarterly require about 30% of every dollar you make be tucked away. When you add in additional costs like health insurance, cell phone bill and renting a conference room or workspace, well, it adds up quickly!

In addition to working for clients under AB and C, I picked up several of my own clients, and three other agencies hired me to help support their clients. I was busy, so very busy, but I was also broke. I made the mistake of working with small businesses who had very little budget (I worked out several of these relationships in partial trade), and being responsible for a strategy that heavily involved local media relationships, of which I had few, since most of my work had been with editors in New York.

Through a series of events, many of my clients were forced to cut PR budgets altogether, and eventually I went back to work for yet another PR agency. I went back to agency life because for the opportunity to be the key PR contact to help launch an upscale women's boutique in town. This was a crash course in event planning, local media relations and resulted in a fabulous launch party for which we closed down the street and built a runway in the middle of it! But, that is a story for another time.

Starting Your Own Agency

If you do decide to strike out on your own, heed the following advice from Lauren Rich. In December 2006, Lauren graduated magna cum laude with a degree in Advertising + Marketing Communications from FIT, and launched RICHPR that same month with two clients she gained while still in school. For the last 3+ years, she has successfully grown RICHPR into a thriving Fashion, Accessories & Lifestyle PR Agency.

Lack of experience can only hold you back if you're not a) motivated and b) resourceful. Make the most of every internship, position, project, opportunity that comes your way. Ask questions, work hard, make contacts, and take on as much responsibility as you can. I lucked out in getting an amazing internship the summer before I graduated, where I met two of my greatest mentors and really learned the ropes of PR. By the time I graduated I had two clients in tow and basically took a leap of faith. Given I had no prior agency experience beyond internships, I really had to rely on instinct and common sense to basically make up my own rules as I went along. Sure, I definitely made some mistakes that 1st year, but you know what – you learn from them, grow stronger, and keep going.

If there's one thing I've learned it's that there is no set way to do things. Just because one agency does something one way does not mean you have to do it the same way. Think outside of the box, find what works for you, and stick with it. Being an entrepreneur can be a lonely world if you have no one to bounce ideas off of, so be sure to surround yourself with others in the industry to build a support base. How to find this support base? Network, network, network. And although this may sound cliché, follow the Golden Rule – be nice to people and help others out, and they will be nice back to you and help you out.
Lack of experience can only inhibit you if you show it. If you arrive to a meeting nervous and doubting yourself, the client will sense it. Stay strong and confident, and where you lack in experience prove you can make up in motivation, creativity and resourcefulness. Most importantly – stay optimistic. If a client doesn't work out or a press

hit doesn't come through, do not feel defeated. You are going to have both achievements and pitfalls, and you have to be able to let go of the negatives and focus on the positives.

Showroom

Working in a showroom provides exposure to buyers and stylists. Lauren Applebaum, Founder & Principal Consultant at LRA PR and Marketing and Media Relations at Sherson Group / Nine West in Toronto provides the skinny on showroom life:

Working PR in a large-scale fashion showroom is not like being a sales rep. At Sherson Group, for example, our fashion portfolio includes Nine West Canada, for example, encompasses a wholesale and retail division. Each brand represented has its own separate showroom (such as Nine West footwear, Nine West handbags, etc.). There is also a fashion closet for marketing specific samples.

It will be your job to manage the PR of showroom and fashion closet samples. This includes selecting styles for editorial exposure (such as magazines, newspapers, television spots, mall events, fashion shows & fashion events, etc.).

Organization is crucial when working with an abundance of samples and this will be a significant part of your job. The samples may be organized in a number of different ways such as alphabetically, by buying market, and/or by trend, etc. They may also be stickered and/or labeled accordingly. Managing and tracking the inventory is extremely important. You must always know which styles have been sent out, where they are and when they will be returned. It is imperative to note important company events (tradeshows, fashion shows, major meetings, etc.) to ensure all relevant samples are available in the showrooms. Unfortunately, samples are sometimes returned in poor condition or not returned at all. It will be your responsibility to follow up with stylists and editors about these samples to ensure their safe return to the showroom.

There are certainly many options and different ways to incorporate elements of public relations into your work. When first starting out, gain as much varied experience as possible in order to figure out which set-up works best for you.

Title & Salary

Fashion PR is perceived as a glamorous industry, and for those lucky few handed down a position through well, nepotism, sure, it can instantly be a lucrative career filled with parties and swag. For most of us, however, the rise through the ranks is never going to be one of summers spent in the Hampton's with a wardrobe to rival that of Samantha Jones.

Entry-level salaries are low, positions are competitive, and turnover is high. That said, if you can work through to a senior management position, command an impressive hourly rate as a consultant, or open an agency, the sky really is the limit. In-house salaries tend to be a bit higher at junior and midlevel, but expect entry-level salaries start around $30-35k (my first PR job I made $10 an hour, wince). Experienced publicists pull upwards of $50-70k and top-level salary ranges push six figures and well beyond.

The standard fashion PR agency titles vary, but here is a generic trajectory of titles based on years of experience:

- Fashion PR Intern: 0-2 years' experience
- Account Coordinator (AC): 1-2 years' experience
- Assistant Account Executive (AAE): 2-4 years' experience
- Account Executive (AE): 3-4 years' experience
- Senior Account Executive (SAE): 4-6 years' experience
- Account Manager (AM): 5+ years' experience

- Senior Account Manager (SAM): 5-7 years' experience
- Account Director (AD): 7+ years' experience
- Senior Account Director (SAD): 7-10 years' experience
- Fashion/Division Director: 10+ years' experience
- VP, Fashion Division: 12+ years' experience
- President, Fashion Division: 12+ years' experience

EDUCATION

What should I major in to pursue a career in fashion PR?

Now that you have a handle on what to expect from a career in fashion PR, the next step, much like a newly minted Charlie's Angel, is to gain education and experience in the field. After all, there is no better way to confirm that this career is (or isn't!) right for you, than to learn about public relations and communication theory, paired with some real-world experience.

> *Do I think it's good to go to school to get a communications degree? If you want me to answer honestly, not really. It's a craft and it's something you have to learn by watching other people do.*
>
> *- Kelly Cutrone. Owner, People's Revolution, (INC.com)*

Fashion PR isn't one of those industries where you need to have a specific degree to ensure entry, however strong communication and writing skills are a must. If your university offers a public relations program, by all means start there. However, by also taking classes in business, marketing, journalism, writing, graphic design, web design and advertising, you will get a broader sense of how PR fits into the overall mix.

Web and social media skills are becoming incredibly important; being able to demonstrate your expertise and comfort level with different blogs platforms, Search Engine Optimization (SEO) as well as basic HTML and SCC are smarts way to differentiate yourself from other job applicants.

From a fashion perspective, it's a good idea to learn basic clothing terminology (peter pan collar, A-line, bias-cut) as well as fabrics. In addition, an understanding of fashion history and can only help with putting into context how fashion influences and reflects society at large. The decision to pursue your bachelor's at a traditional four-year university as opposed to a fashion school should most likely depend on what you are looking to get out of your college experience. For example, as a college freshman I knew I liked fashion but I was also interested in international relations, art and film. By going to a small, Liberal-arts College I was able to take classes in everything from Latin American plays to modern dance. When it came time to study abroad I chose to go to the London College of Fashion to study fashion marketing & merchandising.

A Fashion school will offer a focused and specialized experience, while a University will offer a broader perspective with the opportunity to select a focus. Look at the location of the program within the institution - is it in the Art/Design College, Communications, Business? Programs located in each of these colleges will have very different missions, content delivery, and expected outcomes. Find a major you are passionate about and look for courses that help you understand the big picture - Economics, International Business, Global Marketing and Promotion. Try to get at least one Study Abroad experience.

Embrace technology and learn how to leverage your personal skills into business. Take online courses that help you develop self-directed learning, collaboration and online presentation skills. These will be crucial to success in the future.

– Anne Cecil, Director, Design & Merchandising, AW College of Media Arts & Design, Drexel University

I have taught PR courses at both FIDM and the Art Institute and enjoyed being able to teach like-minded students with a singular focus. However, I personally still favor gaining a broader education and exploring multiple academic pursuits – after all, you may stumble upon a discipline you had never been exposed to in high school and fall in in total nerd love with a new subject. However, the networking opportunities and ability to learn about the fashion industry from the inside out at a fashion school is invaluable, especially for those who are sure that the fashion industry is the right place to at least begin a career.

12 US Colleges & Universities with a Fashion PR Program (or equivalent)

1. American Intercontinental University (BFA, Fashion Marketing)
2. Art Institute (BA, Fashion Marketing)
3. Berkeley College (BS, Fashion Marketing & Management)
4. Columbia College (BA, Fashion Marketing)
5. LIM College (BA, Marketing)
6. FIDM (BA, Business Management, Merchandising)
7. FIT (BA, Advertising and Marketing Communications)
8. University of Missouri (BA, Fashion Marketing)
9. Northwood University (BA, Fashion Marketing & Management)
10. Sacred Heart University (BA, Fashion Marketing)
11. Syracuse University (BA, Public Relations with a concentration in fashion and beauty communications)
12. Woodbury College (BA, Fashion Marketing)

10 Top Public Relations Universities

1. University of Alabama
2. Bradley University
3. Emerson College
4. James Madison University
5. University of Maryland
6. University of Miami
7. New York University (NYU)
8. University of Oregon
9. University of Southern California (USC)
10. San Diego State University

Programs have not been vetted. For informational purposes only.

INTERNSHIPS

How important are internships, and how do I find them?

Gaining work experience is absolutely crucial to launching a fashion PR career. Crucial. If you can, intern at a different PR agency or communications type job every semester until you graduate. Not only is this essential networking for future job opportunities and an opportunity to see how different agencies operate, but the work you do during your internships is essential for building your portfolio.

Kent State has the #3 fashion design school in the country. I started working with TOMS my sophomore year of college and helped establish Ohio's first TOMS Campus Club. I managed all Integrated Marketing Communications (IMC) efforts on campus. We also had a Rock Your TOMS show and I worked with local musicians to have various benefit concerts for TOMS.

Kent State's campus club was the first in Ohio, so I ended up visiting other universities and teaching them how to start their own campus clubs. I created online print advertisements and social media campaigns to increase meeting and event attendance. Our club received 2010 Spirit of Service Award and 2010 New Service Initiative for marketing efforts and entrepreneurial success of organization.

After working with TOMS, I began interning with L'OREAL and really fell in love with fashion and lifestyle PR. My advice to anyone looking to get into fashion is to start NOW. There are always reasons to procrastinate, but my entire career has come out of starting the TOMS campus club because I loved the shoes and the cause.

– Brianne Kimmel, Account Executive, Apparent

One of the best things I did during college was take classes in anything and everything that interested me. Horror Films? Check. Visions of the Divine Feminine? Check. Creative Nonfiction? Check. College was a time to absorb and explore anything and everything that piqued my interest. However, if I could go back and do it all over again, I would have devoted at least part of my time to gaining as much real-world work experience as possible. Unfortunately, I was more focused on ensuring that I made all the work-study money allotted to me as part of my scholarship, and only managed to acquire a single summer internship during my four-years (the now defunct women's lifestyle site called Chicklick.com).

If you, like me, made it through college not knowing you wanted to work in fashion PR and have no internship experience, not to worry. Just know that you might need to have both a fashion PR internship and a paying job for a few months, in order to get this experience. Virtual internships (where you work from home, often for an agency based elsewhere) are a great way to be able to continue to make money, while dedicating your nights, weekends and downtime to helping a fashion PR company, proximity not required!

Intern Responsibilities

I'm a student at UGA and work for Creative Consultants, a student-run PR firm within the University of Georgia's PRSSA chapter. Rent the Runway is one of Creative Consultants' clients. My responsibilities include driving sign ups, acting as the liaison with our salon partners, planning and hosting events. I also pitch story ideas to local magazines and newspapers to bring awareness to rent the Runway locally.

- Nicole McClellan, Jr. Account Executive, Rent the Runway

While it certainly varies, below are a variety of tasks often performed at the intern or entry-level.

- Attend client and media meetings
- Compile status reports
- Build media lists
- Identify award and speaking opportunities
- Manage event RSVP's and guest entry
- Manage client or agency social media accounts
- Monitor and pitch media
- Secure editorial calendars
- Send out samples to media
- Track press coverage
- Write press releases

How to Find Fashion PR Internships

The hardest part of completing internships is landing the first one. Always make use of your university's career center and job board.

Internship Websites
- Creative Jobs Central
- Fashionista
- Free Fashion Internships
- Hoo Jobs
- InternQueen
- InternMatch
- PR Couture Job Board
- Student Jobs
- UC Davis TXC and FPS Internships

Recruiters

Interns and entry-level applicants may also find success by working with staffing and recruitment agencies. There are handfuls that specialize in the fashion and entertainment industries.

- Atrium Staffing
- Fourth Floor Fashion
- Keva Dine
- Twenty-Four Seven

Work Your Network

Reach out to your network; you never know if your former co-worker's sister's fiancé happens to do PR for Steve Madden. Take every opportunity to let people know you are looking - the gym, church, your parent's boring dinner party – when the inevitable "what's new," or "what's going on in your life," question comes up, let anyone and everyone know you are looking to gain experience in public relations, ideally in the fashion industry.

Social Media

Sites like Twitter and LinkedIn are great ways to discover job opportunities. On Twitter, search for hashtags including #PRJobs, #PRIntern, #intern, #internship, #PR101, and follow @EntryPRJobs, @PRJobs and @FindInternships.

On LinkedIn, make sure your profile is up-to-date and includes at least three recommendations. Join groups for PR and fashion industry professionals.

While you wait for your dream job to present itself, you can build your portfolio by taking on small jobs writing press releases, media kits, etc. through sites like Guru and Elance or even Fiverr.

Many fashion PR agencies also have Facebook pages and post job openings. "Like" several fashion PR agencies to stay up to date on company news and opportunities. Comment thoughtfully and consistently on what they share to get noticed.

Professional Organizations

If you are a student, the PRSSA provides networking and access to job boards, as does PRSA. Fashion Group International (FGI) can also be a smart investment. If you don't have a fashion networking group in your town, why not start one? In San Diego, we have Fashion Opportunities Connect Us (FOCUS), which connects fashion professionals through educational events.

Agency Contact Information

Many of the top fashion PR agencies are known for being rather tight-lipped, their websites nothing more than landing pages with a phone number and email address. To find out the right contact for internships and entry-level positions, gather your courage and call up the agency (this is a time when calling is better than email). Ask for the name and email address of the person in charge of internships.

Most often, PR agencies looks for internships each semester/season (fall, spring, and summer), and post job openings 1-3 months in advance. Additionally, many fashion PR agencies need extra help during fashion week (September and February). Helping out for a few weeks leading up to fashion week can be a crash course in fashion PR – comb Craigslist for many of these postings.

Top Fashion PR Agencies

Below are twenty fashion PR agencies headquartered in New York and ten based in Los Angeles. Visit http://prcouture.com/readytolaunch and enter the password "Success," for agency contact information.

New York

Alison Brod Public Relations
- Website: http://www.alisonbrodpr.com

Bismarck Phillip
- Website: http://www.bpcm.com

Factory PR
- Website: http://www.factorypr.com

Harriet Weintraub (HWPR)
- Website: http://www.hwpr.com

Harrison and Shriftman
- Website: http://hs-pr.com

HL Group
- Website: http://www.hlgrp.com

Industry Publicity
- Website: http://www.industrypublicity.com

KCD Worldwide
- Website: http://www.kcdworldwide.com

Krupp Group
- Website: http://kruppgroup.com

LaForce + Stevens
- Website: http://www.laforce-stevens.com

Lippe Taylor
- Website: http://www.lippetaylor.com

Loving & Company
- Website: http://lovingandcompany.com

Nadine Johnson
- Website: http://www.nadinejohnson.com

Regan Communications, Fashion Division
- Website: http://regancomm.com

Pierce Mattie PR
- Website: http://www.piercemattie.com

PR Consulting
- Website: http://www.prconsulting.net

People's Revolution
- Website: http://peoplesrevolution.com

Shadow PR
- Website: http://shadowpr.com

Starworks Group
- Website: http://starworksgroup.com

Style House PR
- Website: http://www.stylehousepr.com

Los Angeles

Bollare Communications
- Website: http://www.bollare.com

BPCM LA
- Website: http://www.bpcm.com

Chic Little Devil PR
- Website: http://cldstylehouse.com/pr

Elle Communications
- Website: http://ellecomm.com

Eileen Koch & Company
- Website: http://www.eileenkoch.com

Feinstein/McGuiness PR
- Website: http://www.fmpr.tv

Michelle Marie PR
- Website: http://michellemariepr.com

Much and House PR
- Website: http://muchandhousepr.com

Samantha Slaven Publicity
- Website: http://samanthaslaven.com

P3R
- Website: http://myp3r.com

How to Make Your Application Stand Out

Before you even think about applying, make sure to read the job posting carefully. If the posting says no attachments, don't send your resume as an attachment. If the posting says put "Spring Intern" in the email subject, make sure to do so.

> *One thing I always do: at the very end of the job posting, I specify a resume, cover letter AND favorite dessert. It's mostly a test that the candidate is interested enough in the job to read the posting thoroughly and is able to follow directions, but also gives a glimpse into their personality.*
>
> *- Melanie Bender, Partner, Post + Beam*

Resume

Consider the roles and responsibilities required for the position like clues on a treasure hunt. Examine your resume and look for places where you can clarify your previous experience using those same words. Use action verbs – coordinated, managed, secured and whenever possible focus on the results of those actions. How many people attended the fashion show? How many people followed the Twitter account under your management?

Cover Letter

Write a cover letter that demonstrates that you have read the job posting. Use examples to demonstrate your experience and skill as it relates to the specific responsibilities outlined in the post.

If you ensured that local media attended a boutique opening for example, call out that you not only have existing relationships with local media, but that several of them attending the last event you worked on. If you have a fashion blog and recently worked with a brand on a campaign, showcase that you understand the needs of both bloggers and brands and highlight that as an area of distinction and expertise. If you minored in economics or finance, highlight how those skills allow you to develop plans that work within client budgets. And please, allow your personality to come through, no one likes to read a boring cover letter!

> *If you're going to work in fashion PR, yes, we want to know that you llloooovvveee fashion, but understand that loving fashion is only one part of the industry. We always say that "working" in fashion is...well, "working" in fashion. It requires the same basic skill sets that other employers require and it's not all sparkle and glamour.*
>
> *- Nancy Vaughn, Principal, White Book Agency*

Go Digital

Showcase those in-demand social media and web skills by linking to a virtual (or video) resume. Include a QR code or shortlink that links to a video of you talking directly about why you are excited (and qualified) for the position.

10 Ways to Land Your First Fashion PR Job

Below are ten different examples of how PR practitioners landed their first fashion PR job. One thing is for sure; it's time to start using Twitter!

1. Coach

I was studying Fashion Management post-grad in Toronto, trying to take as much on in terms of volunteer opportunities and internships in the Canadian fashion industry. I had to complete a full-time summer internship and knew that New York City would be the best place to get my start and a better sense of what the Fashion PR industry held on an international level.

My best friend from Canada had been working in PR in NYC for a couple of years and kindly reached out to one of his contacts in Coach's PR department who introduced me to their internship coordinator. I started as a summer intern and treated it as if it were a full-time job. At the end of that summer I became an assistant in the PR department. I later moved on to a fashion PR agency and in early 2009 formed my own firm specializing in fashion accessories - taking the strengths from both in-house and agency structures. I learned a lot from my very first full-time PR experience and even became close friends with my former internship coordinator and other Coach colleagues.

– Liz Anthony, CEO, Mariposa Communications

2. Elevate PR

I started to follow people [on Twitter] with similar interests, and began networking online. That is when I met Audrey Huynh of Elevate PR. We started conversing over Twitter about celebrities, fashion, and life in Southern California. After a while, our relationship grew to a point where it was like we already knew each other. Eventually, Audrey offered me an internship with Elevate PR, and of course I accepted!

- Bonny Park

3. xPose PR

I tirelessly stalked multiple internship websites an internship post for at xPose PR. After researching the company and their vibe, I wrote a specific cover letter that I believed embodied xPose. I must have done something right because a couple days later, I received an email asking if I was available for an interview.

- Jessica Oakes

4. Melbourne Spring Fashion Week

I found my current agency job by connecting with a Sydney ad agency long before I graduated from college. I'm a digital strategist and my major client is Nikon. Recently, I worked on Nikon's campaign for Melbourne Spring Fashion Week and positioned Nikon as the premier camera for the fashion industry.

- Brianne Kimmel

5. White Book Agency

During my time volunteering at Tampa Bay Fashion Week I worked really hard to impress Nancy from White Book Agency, and my efforts definitely paid off. The following week she phoned me and asked if I wanted to meet for an interview, and here I am!

- Maggie Philbin

6. Claire's Inc.

I received an email from the Vice President of Claire's Marketing. He was interested in me due to my Linkedin Profile.

- Jennifer Lezan

7. The Contact List

At San Jose State University they require you to intern at a company for credit before you can graduate. I interned at 944 Magazine in San Francisco - a 3-hour commute by train every morning from my apartment in San Jose! While playing around on Twitter during the train ride, I came across an internship posting on Twitter from *The Contact List.* They were looking for interns to help make calls to make sure the company contact database was current. I applied even though I was not local. I explained my situation and that I was willing to make all their East Coast calls since I was commuting at 6am, which is prime time for NYC calls. I continued to make calls through the summer and when school started I was able to work with *The Contact List* to continue my internship on a smaller scale.

In October, *The Contact List* helped to put on the LA Fashion Week Opening Gala at the Standard Hotel and they needed interns for the event so they flew me down. It was the first time I met my boss in person! I continued to keep an open relationship with *The Contact List* while I was in school and they flew me out for a few fashion week events. The February before graduation I began applying to jobs in Los Angeles and made it very clear with *The Contact List* that I was interested in joining the team locally. That April they offered me a position and I relocated in June. I know without a doubt that is was my persistence, drive and work ethic that got me the full time position with *The Contact List* after graduation.

- Rachel Meiss, Rachel Meis Communications

8. Circa PR

In one of my public relations classes I had to interview the founder of a public relations firm for an essay. I knew Circa PR specialized in fashion and retail so Katie Kern was the perfect fit. After the interview I was very interested in an internship with Circa PR and asked Katie if she ever needed an intern to contact me. Luckily, she did and here I am!

- Carter Boardman

9. Dream Cartel PR

Dream Cartel PR actually reached out to me and let me know about this opportunity via Twitter. I frequently tweet about fashion and PR and caught their attention. My professors are always telling us to use

Twitter to make connections and network with industry professionals, and I am so glad I listened. I am a huge proponent of social media (especially Twitter) as it helped me to land this great internship.

- Lindsay Bailey

10. Von Dutch

Fashion PR was a happy accident for me. I was always a music guy. I was the lead singer of a rock band in college and that's what I wanted to do with my life, so my first job out of college was at The Firm. After doing that for a few years, I got tired of the state of the music industry and went to interview at Von Dutch. I had always liked fashion, but never really thought of it as a profession. Once I started working at Von Dutch, it came very natural to me to style celebrities and do fashion PR. I never really planned it, but things have a funny way of working themselves out.

– Chris Detert, CEO American Rebel PR

Make the Most of Your Internship

Once you've landed the haute spot - don't get lazy or start daydreaming in the shoe closet. Make your internship work for you. How? Work on developing the following five key attributes that will serve you well in your career.

Being willing to pitch in wherever needed and showing initiative is a great way to win over your new team. It takes time and effort to train people, so often in busy environments like PR, the best way to learn is to jump right in there.

I look for someone who is positive, excited to be there and willing to do anything. Starting at the bottom in PR means picking up samples, clipping press, organizing, making copies, and even getting coffee at times- the enthusiasm someone shows for these menial tasks is what gets you to the next level.

– Leah Jacobson, Director of PR, Elie Tihari

Ask Questions

At entry-level, there is no benefit to act like you know more, or have done more, than you do. If you have a tendency to "embellish" a little, don't. Show your enthusiasm for clients, projects and tasks and demonstrate quick thinking and learning rather than pretending you understand something you don't. It may sound counterintuitive, but asking questions and admitting you don't know something is an attractive quality in a potential employee! It's all right to still be learning, especially in an intern role or entry-level position.

Have an Opinion

Don't be afraid to apply what you learn in class or to ask questions, doing so shows that you are paying attention! Thinking critically shows your intelligence, dedication and eagerness to learn– all qualities that employers love. Looking for problem solving opportunities and take on responsibility to solidify yourself as a valuable employee and team player. This is your time to learn as much as you can, so make the most of it. If you want press releases to add to your portfolio, ask to take first crack at a new client release. If you want to know how new business presentations are given, ask to sit in on a pitch. If you want to understand the PR strategy, ask to participate in a brainstorming session.

Build and Maintain Relationships

Skilled publicists are natural connectors. We love coming up with ways to bring the people we know together for combined success; after all, relationships are the foundation of public relations. Maintaining, nurturing and growing relationships with media, co-workers, partners, vendors, and then leveraging those relationships on behalf of clients successfully is what sets you apart and builds your reputation. Relationships drive what you can accomplish, whether it's a quick phone call to secure a morning show appearance, or partnership with a graphic designer you can depend on for a quick-turn around when the season preview invites get lost in the mail.

During your internship, keep every business card and write notes on the back or keep a word doc with what might come in handy later (from Rhode Island, Mom is a florist, 5yr old daughter, Charlie). Impress everyone you come into contact with by being positive, professional, resourceful and fun to work with.

> **Tip:** Stay in touch with those you meet by sending a quarterly email to potential future job employers, former colleagues, people you met at a networking event, that kind of thing. Give them an update on what you are up to, any recent successes, anything you are looking for (from a job to a web developer), and ask them to please send you an update as well. Staying connected to those you meet along the way can have very beneficial consequences down the line!

Upgrade Your Communication Skills

Publicists must be able to clearly communicate across multiple forms of media, from writing a press release to cold calling an editor. Strategic thinking and creativity leads to powerful campaign ideas and pitches, which then need to be developed and personalized for each target, be it the local business journal or a tweet.

When speaking with an editor or entertaining media at an event, it is important to be well prepared, personable, and to personalize conversation to the media's interest. Eavesdrop when the Account Exec in the next cube over is speaking to the beauty editor at *Nylon*, listen to her tone and the way she shares information about her client. Say yes to any opportunity to write or pitch yourself, and make sure to ask for feedback about your efforts. You may want to record yourself when doing any pitching to see how you sound – are you tentative, do you use terms like "like," "you guys," or "you know," a lot? Make a concerted effort to work on your speech patterns.

When it comes to written communication, review press releases, pitches and media alerts being sent out by your company, as well as emails back and forth with clients. Paying special attention to the headline, the way the information is organized and the overall tone.

Fake it Till You Make it

Public Relations is not for the faint of heart. You must find a way to thrive under pressure, to be able to come up with ideas for anything and everything, and then, essentially sell others on your idea. After a few hours of calling editors and not getting anywhere, it can be discouraging. On top of this, many PR agencies can be hectic, high-stress places, not to mention the office politics that plague any office. During your internship and likely for the first few years of your career, you will make mistakes. It's unavoidable. It is what you do with your mistakes, how you react, how you fix them, and how you are able to never make the same one twice, that will define you.

My first week at the jewelry company, I put the wrong 800-number into an email that went out to hundreds of thousands of customers. Oh the embarrassment. Instead of beating yourself up when you accidentally misspell or mispronounce an editor's name, take a deep breath and give yourself a big hug. It happens to everyone. The key is to acknowledge every oops and thank that oops for teaching you something new (like to triple check a phone number, or ask a co-worker if you are unsure if it is Ahhhndrea or Aaaandrea).

Ask for Feedback

It's important that you get the professional experience and support you need from your internship, particularly when you are working for school credit. Make sure that you are getting regular feedback from your boss and peers. After completing a project, ask for feedback. "I really enjoyed working on this project. I'd appreciate any suggestions you have to help me improve for next time. Do you have fifteen minutes this week to touch base?"

Open the lines of communication by sharing the parts of the position you are finding valuable, and then constructively approach the areas where you are struggling. Make a clear request – "I'd like for us to meet weekly to review my to-dos – is that possible?" Or, "I'd like to receive some training on Photoshop in order to be able to do these clips faster." You may even want to bring in a well-researched plan on how to implement a more formal internship program (for example!

One final note: Your time is valuable. If you don't feel like the internship meets your expectations, feel lost or unclear about what you should be doing, or how you are doing, ask for a meeting with your boss.

INTERVIEWS

How can I rock my interview?

So you landed an interview – congrats! This alone means that your resume, cover letter and social media presence are "dressed to impress." Further impress your interviewer by demonstrating your enthusiasm and professionalism. Arrive 5-10 minutes early, with extra copies of your resume, business cards, something to write on and with. Make full use of body language - eye contact, smiles and nods to show you are paying attention and listening. Demonstrate that you have done your research on the company and have a few specific career wins to share, even if it is just a volunteer experience or a leadership role you assumed for a recent school project. Remember, your interviewer has a problem – there is a position that needs to be filled, work that needs to get done. Be the problem-solver and communicate exactly why you are the solution.

> *We do a little media 'quiz' in our interviews...it really helps weed out those who really know the fashion/design/beauty media and those who don't! We have questions about magazines (which have folded and which haven't!), key people are in the fashion/design worlds and which outlets they think would be good fits for our clients. We also ask what they know about our clients. It's a good indicator of someone who has done his or her 'homework' before the interview.*
>
> *- Melissa Davis, Founder, Ruby Press*

Never say anything negative about a former employer and frame any difficult experiences in a positive light. Speak to the point at hand, keeping any rambling or long-winded stories to a minimum. At the end of your interview, be sure to end on a strong, confident note! Reiterate your interest, enthusiasm and excitement for the opportunity. Remind your interviewer why you are a fit for the position and indicate you are looking forward to next steps.

Bring a Portfolio

When [applicants] show me their portfolio, I ask questions about who they worked with. For example, if they show me a clip from WWD, after they've turned to the next page, I'll ask, "Whom did you work with on that WWD piece?" That way I know if their portfolio was really their work or part of their larger teams. I always ask them to walk me through the process of pitching a story to the media, as well to be sure I don't have a spammer on my hands!

- Danielle Gano, Founder, Elle Communications

As you move along in your career, you will no doubt be placing clips, press kits, invites etc. from the amazing work you are doing into your portfolio. If you don't currently have any work samples, be creative. Publish pieces in your student or city newspaper, magazines, or blog and put those in your portfolio. Create a company newsletter for your job, or work with your creative friends and a local boutique to create and then promote a seasonal photo shoot. Build a press kit for your friend who is a model/jewelry designer, or write a faux fashion PR plan for a company you admire. Classroom examples of press releases or media alerts are also great, as examples of brochures you designed, or an article you submitted to a local site. Of course, if you have done PR before, include any results - screenshots or actual clips of media coverage you have secured. The goal is to demonstrate your initiative, creative thinking and writing skills.

When you have several samples ready, find a binder you like (mine is red canvas), pick up some sheet protectors, and begin to assemble a clean, organized portfolio. Begin with your resume and bio, perhaps even a fun "10 things about me," to personalize it further. Then, in order of most recent, dive into the examples.

It's also a smart idea to have these samples stored digitally on your own website. Include the link to your online portfolio in your thank you email so that your work can be easily shared among the decision-makers.

What to Wear

While there are no hard and fast rules about what to wear to a fashion PR interview - aside from the obvious - it's always better to over-dress than under-dress. And, this is fashion, so let your personal sense of style shine through.

Ladies: You can never go wrong with a nicely tailored suit – it shows you take the job and your professional career seriously. However, do a bit of research on the agency culture. To a lifestyle firm with a casual dress code, for example, a basic suit might read as boring, unimaginative and overdone. Instead, think about separates – a solid black pencil skirt with a patterned blouse, or a flattering full skirt with a pattern, paired with a solid basic top. Also, you can never go wrong with a simple wrap dress. Unique accessories like a bold necklace or an unexpected shoe color are also great ways to infuse a bit of personality into your look. Remember to remove any chipped nail polish and to make sure any perfume is sprayed lightly, there's nothing quite like finding out your interviewer is allergic or hates the smell of rose.

For menswear, I enlisted the advice of fashion PR pro Michael Shane Stephens:

It's easy to get lost in the crowd with the rest of the suits. In fashion PR, it is imperative that your style stands out. Unlike other professions, in fashion PR, the adage you are what you wear holds true. At least when it comes to making a first impression. When dressing for an interview, think tailoring. Everything on a man should be tailored to fit your body.

Invest in a well-tailored suit. If you're on a budget, honestly, H&M Slim Fit suits work perfectly, and at around $250, are great options. If you're going out for a senior level position, you should already own at least one tailored, Italian wool suit. The suit color is not as important as your shirt, tie, shoes and other accessories.

We know how hard it is for men to accessorize, but it can be done. The shirt should pop, as it, along with the tie, is your pièce de résistance. Go for bold colors and textures, gingham, check, or stripes will do the trick. Offset this with an opposite colored/ patterned tie or simply go solid. Or vice versa... a solid colorful shirt with a bold patterned, skinny tie. And finally, the shoes. Again, go the distance and invest in something that will get noticed such as a nice pair of wingtips. You won't think so but the tinniest details do get noticed. If you can pull it off, throw on a bow tie. A real one, NOT a clip on. This is the ultimate men's fashion accessory.

20 Fashion PR Job Interview Questions

Figuring out what to wear to your interview is stressful. But what's worse is fumbling bumbling your way through a curve ball question you weren't expecting. So, I asked several fashion PR agencies owners to share their favorite interview questions. You're welcome!

Tip: Ask a bestie to run through these with you and pretend you are running lines for the next chick flick starring you and your new fancy fashion PR job! If you get nervous or stumble, choose an actress you would have play you, and pretend you are her, delivering the best response possible, about you. You know, for the movie about your life!

- What is it about PR that makes this profession your "dream job?"
- How would you say social media has changed the way we communicate in the past couple years? How do you think it's affected PR and how we work with the media?
- What do you know about our company?
- Who is your favorite designer, both high fashion & street?
- What's your favorite thing in your closet and why?
- What blogs do you follow on a daily basis?
- Tell me about a time you worked well under pressure?
- What do you expect or appreciate from a boss?
- If you were hiring for this position, what qualities would you look for?
- What parts of your education do you see are relevant to this position?
- What are you really good at professionally?
- What are you not good at or not interested in doing professionally?

- Describe a situation in which you used persuasion to convince someone to see things your way.
- Describe a time when you were faced with a stressful situation that demonstrated your coping skills.
- Give me a specific example of a time when you used good judgment and logic in solving a problem.
- Tell me about a time when you had to go above and beyond the call of duty in order to get a job done.
- Tell me about a time when you had too many things to do and you were required to prioritize your tasks.
- Tell me about a difficult decision you've made in the last year.
- Tell me three things you would improve about our website.
- How would you define public relations?

12 Questions to Ask During the Interview

At some point during the interview, you will undoubtedly be asked if you have any questions. Instead of shaking your head, use this as an opportunity to further demonstrate why you are an excellent candidate. Whatever you do, don't ask questions that are clearly answered on the company website or in any additional information already provided!

Here are a few great questions to ask (if you're up for an entry-level position, just swap out the word internship for job).

- How do you envision this internship supporting the goals of the company?
- What types of daily tasks will I be responsible for during this internship?
- What type of feedback or review can I expect to get during

my internship?

- What types of mentorship/training can I except to receive during this internship?
- As a manager, tell me about your style? What drives you nuts?
- What are your expectations of me?
- What are the opportunities for career advancement?
- I noticed that you did X for client X, how did that all come about?
- What clients or projects can I expect to work on during this internship?
- How do you measure success for clients?
- What role does social media play in the work you do for clients?
- What are the biggest strengths and areas of expertise of this agency?

Post-Interview Tips

Your performance during the interview is important, sure. But know that your actions post-interview are just as important. Resist any/all urges to Tweet or Facebook about the interview (stay mum on the entire process when it comes to your social profiles) and make sure to be as polite to the receptionist as you were to your interviewer.

Follow-up and Follow Through

Send an immediate thank you email to your contact and follow up with a hand-written note the next day. In the email, demonstrate your communication skills and provide links to articles or previous work that came up during the interview. Be genuine and establish a personal connection.

If you interviewed with several people, send a unique card with unique content to each person. If you can, thank each person for something specific they shared with you.

Finally, make sure to triple-check your thank you notes for grammar and spelling. A mistake in your thank you note will likely cost you the job – so make sure that everything looks good (have someone else look it over just to be extra sure) and that contact names are spelled correctly.

Tip: Ask for a few names and phone numbers of former interns – catching a quick cup of coffee with someone who has been through the experience can help you make sure the position is a fit.

Informational Interviews

The best approach to landing an informational interview is to kill 'em with kindness and fatten' 'em with flattery! If possible, find something or someone you have in common (marathons, marathon shopping, zodiac sign, or PETA) and lead with that. Then ask for a quick 10 minutes on the phone to send a short list of questions via email. Make sure you profess your profound gratitude afterwards. When you do 'land' your job, drop a note with the news and how much their input helped to put you on the map. You never know, one day, that fellow marathoner might call and offer you a job.

- Shannon Cavanagh-Estrada, Co-Founder, Pitch! Press

If there are no current job openings listed, do not send a one-sentence email from your phone asking if there are any jobs available (yes, that happens!). Instead, treat this communication like you would a cover letter for a job that did exist; outline your experience, interest and what about your skills make you a great candidate. Indicate that you are interested in being considered for potential openings in the future.

People love to talk about themselves. It's totally ok to request an informational interview or phone call to learn more about the agency or brand and see if there is a potential fit. If you can't access anyone at the executive level, speak with an account coordinator or someone with just a few more years experience than you do. After all, she has recently been where you are and may be more willing to spend some time imparting wisdom.

Tip: Don't ask people to lunch or out for drinks. To a busy person, this is a red flag. Ask for 15-20 minutes of their time. If they can't make time for a coffee date, offer to bring the coffee to them and ask them a few questions at their desk. Make it so easy on the person you are looking to connect with that they can't say no!

REPUTATION

How can I best present myself for ongoing career success?

Joan Jett might not have given a damn about her reputation, but that was rock n roll, and this is PR. Just because you don't have to worry about getting Pap'd (new favorite word – aka Paparazzi, not the other thing) while breaking in your new bikini doesn't mean that you aren't being watched. The way you carry yourself in world, and the way you portray yourself matters.

In PR, you are your reputation. Pure and simple.

The good news is that most of the time (barring the occasional batty co-worker or insane boss), you have total control over this. The other good news is that many of the qualities you already possess, the ones that have drawn you to a career in PR, are the very traits that will lead you to be successful. Over time, your resourcefulness, creativity, enthusiasm, and work ethic will provide you with experience, credibility and confidence. Keep at it, and you will become an expert.

Headshots

It's remarkable how many of us, in spite of being in an industry all about image, put up grainy, unflattering, awkwardly cropped photos up on our social media profiles. Instead of cropping yourself out of a sorority formal, or last year's holiday card, invest in headshots. They don't have to be taken by a professional and you don't have to spend a ton of money on them, but make the investment in time to have gorgeous photos taken of yourself. It's a great business asset, and can be really fun.

Grab your best photographer friend and work together to find a few places about town (we call this location scouting) to play photo shoot. Have a friend do your make up or have it done at a make-up counter, wear your hair loose and natural. Choose a few outfits - one professional (toss a blazer on over anything and you've got it), one more casual, and one that really shows off your personal style, and spend an afternoon smizing (that's smiling with your eyes for those uninitiated into *America's Next Top Model),* and working that camera!

Online Reputation Management

We live in the world of the big G. Anything that comes up under a Google search, including a Google image search for your name, blog name, Twitter name, etc. is fair game for a prospective employer to find, review and well, judge. Paying attention to your search results isn't self-importance; it demonstrates proactive, smart business sense. In PR, we call this Reputation Management.

Every comment on a blog post, every photo tagged in a public album, tweet or interview has the potential to live in perpetuity and can be easily seen by hiring managers with a quick Google search.

I review sites like Twitter, Facebook, LinkedIn and the personal blogs of potential employees. I ask myself – how would my clients feel about this person representing them if they were to find the same things I did? That can make the hiring decision very easy. I pay attention to the amount of time they spend using social networks and even the skill and efficiency with which they use them. The results always leave an impression.

– Rachel Kay, Founder/President, Rachel Kay Public Relations

In a recent poll by Reppler, 91% of employers polled said they use social networking sites to screen prospective employees. 69% said they have rejected a candidate because of something they saw on one of these social platforms BUT 68% said they have hired a candidate because of something they saw about them on a social networking site. Put that unavoidable pre-interview Google search to work for you, not against you.

Social Media Profiles

Sites like Facebook and Twitter will often populate the first results from a search engine, so make sure to have active profiles. Create profiles under your name, and make sure that your Facebook privacy settings are set to reveal only what you want them to reveal (for a quick fix, just set everything to friends only). To see what a prospective employer will see when they visit your Facebook page, simply log-out and then take a look at what is showing up.

If you are searching for a job, consider choosing a profile picture that shows off your smile, in bright, natural lighting and stay away from any obvious party shots with your boyfriend cropped out.

Keep your LinkedIn and Twitter public, but your Facebook private. Google yourself regularly to see what comes up. It's good when things come up that show your personality and industry prowess. Posting articles and contributing to blogs that interest you will increase positive search results.

–Janna Meyrowitz-Turner, Founder/President, Style House PR

When in Doubt, Don't Post

Ensuring that your online reputation is credible and reinforces the qualities that make you such a desirable candidate will increase the chances of getting an interview. By demonstrating your interest in PR through social media, especially blogging and LinkedIn, you show a future employer that you understand and appreciate the basics of branding. The way you present yourself on and offline will make a difference when it comes to getting hired. Too often, entry-level candidates use social networks as a place to air grievances, complain and generally behave badly. If you need a place to air your dirty laundry, vent about your job, demonstrate your deep understanding of various expletives, and create a second, private account for trusted friends only. When in doubt, ask yourself if you would be comfortable showing your grandmother, future children or romantic partner what you are about to post/share/do. Works every time!

Twitter as a Branding Tool

When job hunting, think of Twitter like a mini resume and less like a personal ad, i.e. include information in your bio about your job expertise, rather than your obsession with vintage Chanel. Create a

Twitter account using your actual name, (or choose something super relevant to your career goals). Use a great photo of your face (the same or similar to the one your LinkedIn page, website, etc.) so people can begin to recognize you from other places, putting a face to the name.

Twitter Chats

A great way to network on Twitter is to participate in weekly Twitter chats. People get together to discuss a particular topic for an hour or so, tagged with a particular hash tag. Don't miss these; they are a great way to connect with those in the industry!

#journchat - Monday at 8 p.m. EST
An ongoing conversation between journalists, bloggers and PR pros.

#pr20chat - Tuesday at 8 p.m. EST
A weekly conversation about public relations 2.0 and where PR is heading.

#u30pro - Thursday at 8 p.m. EST
A community and chat for ambitious PR professionals under 30.

#prstudchat - Monthly at 8:30 p.m. EST
A conversation between public relations students, educators
and professionals

Leverage LinkedIn

LinkedIn is a social network for professionals, sometimes affectionately called "Facebook for grownups." At my current agency, the information and recommendations you have on your profile are more important than anything on your resume. Here are a few tips for making the most out of LinkedIn:

Use Keywords

Avoid using buzzwords and instead focus on using action verbs to describe the specific successes you have had thus far. Focus on results rather than long lists of tasks. For your headline, indicate that you are looking for a job. Play around with keywords in your headline and expertise and see if the number of people viewing your profile increases as well.

Complete Your Profile

Complete your profile and make sure to have more than one job listed in order to be 12 times more likely to be viewed by job hunters. Students and recent grads can post volunteer work and work experience in a special section, as well as special projects, honors or test score results.

Customize Your URL

Create a custom URL for your profile (mine is LinkedIn/in/crosbynoricks) so that it comes up in a Google search for your name.

Ask for Recommendations

Ask teachers, former employers, colleagues, and students you worked with on projects, etc. to write you a LinkedIn recommendation. In some circles, these recommendations are considered more important than the references you list on your resume.

Increase Your Network

Each time you connect with a potential employer, have a great conversation with someone at a conference, or finish up a project, send that person an invitation to connect on LinkedIn. Over time, you will develop a strong network and you demonstrate immediately your professionalism and understanding of digital networking tools like LinkedIn.

Tip: Instead of just sending the default LinkedIn request, tell the person how you know them and why you want to connect.

Personal Website and Blog

One of the best ways to ensure a professional online presence is to register a website with your name. Provide a bit of information about yourself, including a photo, resume and examples of work experience or college projects. Include your website link on your resume, in the signature line of your email address and in your Twitter bio. You may also want to start a blog.

Consuming PR is not only a creative outlet; it's opened the doors for so many career opportunities. My blog acts as a living portfolio and makes it easy for employers and publications to connect with me beyond my resume.

Consuming PR gives me a leg up on the competition fighting for jobs in this industry and I can honestly say that my blog has helped me land every job on my resume. Blogging demonstrates dedication, writing ability, conceptual thinking and marketing skills. I recommend everyone looking for a job or currently working in public relations to start a blog, you never know where it will take you.

- Sarah Essary, Founder of Consuming PR, Senior Account Executive, Edelman Digital

10 Steps to Successful Blogging

If you decide to start a blog, or you already have one set up but are looking for some tips, here is a crash course in doing it correctly. For more specifics, visit Pro Blogger and Independent Fashion Bloggers.

Own Your Domain

It's not rocket science to install a self-hosted Wordpress blog on its own domain (if I can figure it out, so can you!) and it reads much more professional than using blogspot, onSugar or blog.wordpress.com! If you decide to use Tumblr, consider using it as a supplement to your main blog, like Gala Darling, and whatever you do, make sure to do more than reblog the latest shots from *The Sartorialist*. Demonstrate your originality by producing original content. For a great example of this, check out Jessica Schroeder's *What I Wore*.

Define Your Niche

What do you really enjoy talking about? Are you obsessed with eco-friendly fabrics, runway fashion that looks like renaissance art, or a particular brand or fashion icon – Lululemon or Zandra Rhodes? The blogs that stand out these days explore the old subjects in new ways.

Establish a Brand Aesthetic

The way your blog looks is a direct reflection of you (and on you!) Spend time developing the brand of your blog. Colors, tone, logo and fonts all matter. Consider each carefully.

Develop Recurring Content Themes

Write down as many possible article ideas as you can. Then, take a look at what you have written and note similar themes. It may be DIY craftiness, book reviews, how-tos, or commentary. Group these under thematic headings, and start to plot out categories and recurring content themes.

Create an Editorial Calendar

Once you have your themes, take a look at the month and begin to drop in articles. You may want to do a book review each Wednesday, or a link round up every Friday. Perhaps Mondays are for interviews.

Write for "Scanability"

Blog readers have short attention spans, so use short paragraphs, quotes, and headers to help your reader easily scan your content.

Optimize Article Titles with Keywords

Consider what someone might search for that would land them on your article. Include those words in the title. One of the key ways to drive new readers to your site is to put the words they are searching for into the title of your article. This is why so many articles on PR Couture have "Fashion PR" in the title. A-ha!

Offer to Write Guest Articles

Another great way to build awareness for your blog is to offer to write guest posts on more established blogs. Just shoot your preferred blogger a quick email with information about you, your blog, and a few article ideas you think would be a fit for their site.

Promote Articles via Social Media

Include share buttons on your articles so they can be easily shared by your readers, and make sure you promote your articles on your own social media profiles as well. Instead of just linking to the article, ask a question that invites conversation. And please, do not direct message everyone on your list asking them to please promote your article!

Review Analytics

Your site analytics will tell you what articles are most popular on your site, who is linking to you, and what people are typing into to Google when they find your site. Check them, often.

Keep Going

While it's rare to be an overnight blogging sensation, a commitment to your craft, readers and fellow writers will, over time, set you up for success.

LOCATION

Do I need to move to New York to work in fashion PR?

It's true that fashion happens in every city, no matter how small, and it is possible to get your fashion on pretty much anywhere, especially in the era of virtual internships and email pitching. However, there's nothing quite like being immersed in an epicenter of fashion. At some point you will probably think about moving to New York or LA for your career.

And while sure, you can make a snap decision, pick-up and move, (you're only young once right!) However, knowing what you are getting yourself into first can help better position you for success. For example, I have learned that I don't really like to be around a ton of people all the time, all that go-go-go tires me out. I won't put up with a long commute, and I need to be near water. A mid-size city close to the beach like San Diego is actually a pretty good fit for my deal. I also hate spending obscene amounts of money on food and rent - NY girls I am looking at you! Of course, I give up a lot by being here as well. It's all about crafting a balance you can live with.

To get more of an idea of the pros and cons, I asked someone who just went through the big move to the big apple. Jessica deGuardiola's Boston fashion PR firm, 5sPR, was acquired by Ragan Communications. This required Jessica to relocate to New York to assume a Vice President position with Regan. Here are her thoughts on the matter:

Breaking into the world of fashion PR can seem like a daunting task when first exploring your options. The PR industry as a whole is fast-paced, and when your focus is on fashion, the pressure is only intensified by the fact that most assume the only city to thrive in this world is NY. Luckily, with the increasing popularity of PR as a profession, the surge in online-fashion retailers like Gilt Groupe and Rue La La, and the growth of multi-city fashion hubs around the country like LA and Miami, young hopefuls have more options than one might think.

Having been lucky enough to find a position working in fashion PR in NYC, I could not be more grateful for the experiences I was fortunate enough to have that paved the road in making that happen. My first piece of advice: Start local. If there's a boutique firm in your city, make every effort to break in at an entry level and learn the ropes. It is here that not only will you be allowed the opportunity to make mistakes as you grow (a luxury that is not commonplace in NY) but that you will develop your most valuable contacts and experience, and if nurtured properly, these contacts will last you throughout your career.

Most PR firms nowadays subscribe to one media database or another. Take the time to familiarize yourself with the editors at your favorite fashion magazines. These sites provide a wealth of knowledge that allow you to "get to know" an editor, regardless of your location. Once you've had time to work on your first fashion account and pitch the decision makers that influence what we read on a daily basis, my next suggestion would be to explore the possibility of doing editor desk-sides a few times a year in NYC.

Because NYC is saturated with PR firms, I cannot stress enough the importance of maintaining a regular dialogue with your favorite national editors...and this is made easier when you can put a face to the name and establish a long-term relationship. Of course, this depends on the firm you are working with and your client's budget, but if the opportunity presents itself to arrange 10-15 minute meetings 1 to 2 times a year to go over your client's work and put in "face-time," take full advantage of it! This also is a great way to familiarize yourself with the fashion and media capital of the world, without taking on the burden of breaking into one of the hardest city's possible professionally.

Personally speaking, I'm certain I would not be where I am today had I not started off small, and allowed myself the opportunity to establish not only a name for my firm, but further my relationships with the media without being swallowed alive by jumping the gun and getting lost in the NY shuffle too early in the game. If you're a recent college grad or just simply looking to change professions, take the time to do a little research on what firms are hiring in your area. The hands-on experience will put you light-years ahead and be invaluable for when you're ready to make the leap.

Getting a Move On

Every career journey is unique, but it never hurts to hear from those who have been through it! Below are four more, very different approaches to the "where to live," question.

From Texas to NYC

Moving isn't easy. It's lonely, it's hard, and you have to find your tough, inner self. Sometimes, when people come to New York City they get 'lost.' Sometimes physically, sometimes emotionally, sometimes both. People say, "if you can make it here, you can make it anywhere." I never understood that notion about New York until I moved here. It's true.

New York City is like this living, breathing organism made from steel buildings, harsh winters and bright summers laced in corporations, fast money, culture and wonderment. I moved to New York already having entry-level experience, which I think made my transition into living in such a tough city slightly easier than it could have been, but before I moved here, I was more similar to Andy Sachs in the film, The Devil Wears Prada than anything. Over a year later, I can still hear Miranda Priestly calling me the "wide-eyed girl peddling her earnest newspaper stories!"

You move you may be surrounded by people just as smart as you are, just as ambitious and just as extraordinary. My job hunt was miserable. You can walk into an interview and walk out thinking that you nailed it - you loved them, they loved you and you are without a doubt going to get hired. Then you don't. I believe that the amount of interviews a person goes on has little to do with their level of experience these days and more about being the right fit.

It's not a bad thing to be that wide-eyed girl. It's nice not to be jaded. I appreciate that about myself now. I needed to grow and

New York prepared me for the next phase of my life. After all, I did survive my first year here!

- Sasha H. Muradali, Little Pink Book PR

From Virginia to NYC

I moved to NYC in the summer of 2008 right after graduating with a B.A. in English from Hampton University in Virginia. When I first arrived in NYC, I had no idea what I wanted to do, just that I wanted to write, make money, & be successful!

When I arrived in NYC, I was already blogging on my site, The Loudest Pen Ever, which was a 80s/90s Hip-hop and R&B blog. In the fall of 2009, I attended "Word camp" and met Danielle Holdman, Owner/Publisher of Urbane Perspective Magazine. We then connected on Twitter, which led to an internship at Urbane doing branding/marketing campaigns and writing for the entertainment and fashion sections. I was at Urbane for about a year total when I decided to leave and focus on building my own brand.

I started my fashion site, de la Pen, an international & multicultural fashion, style, beauty, & accessories online publication. Through de la Pen, I have attended and covered multiple fashion events including Style.uz Art Week in Tashkent, Uzbekistan!

Most recently, I co-founded a PR and talent management company, called The Network. We represent emerging ethnic models, stylists, make-up artists, designers, & musicians.

I develop social media marketing campaigns, create press materials like media kits & lookbooks, pitch clients to online editors and bloggers, plan photo shoots and attend events.

I'm still active on de la Pen as well as my new Tumblr, The Blogging PR Girl. I'm always super busy and I have a to-do list for my to-do list. However, I wouldn't trade it for the world because I've had jobs I hated and so I feel blessed to be able to do what I love!

- Candace Newberry, Co-Founder, The Network

From Kansas to NYC

Last summer, I worked for fashion designer Daryl K as a PR intern. Because I had such a great experience, I knew New York was where I wanted to be and fashion PR was what I wanted to do. After graduating from Kansas State in May I moved to New York two weeks later and interviewed with Atrium Staffing. Atrium immediately found me a temporary position at IMG Models as an administrative assistant. After about seven weeks at IMG, they had found a full time replacement so I was back on the job hunt. I contact Fourth Floor Fashion in addition to working with Atrium to find as many opportunities as possible. Through Fourth Floor I interviewed at Monique Pean, Piaget, and Behnaz Sarafpour. Luckily I landed the job at Behnaz Sarafpour, who needed a part-time PR assistant through the end of September. Knowing my temporary position was coming to an end, Fourth Floor contacted me about interviewing at Temple St. Clair, a luxury jewelry designer. Before I even got back to Behnaz's office from the interview, I was offered the job and accepted! After four long months and multiple interviews, I finally have a full time salary job in New York City. Now if I could just find an apartment!

- Dora Maddux, PR Coordinator, Temple St. Clair

From NYC to Los Angeles

Mr. Sinatra was not exaggerating when he sang "if I make it there, I can make it anywhere," New York is the epicenter of well, everything. Whether it's marketing, PR, or events, NYC truly is the ideal place to kick start your career. The experiences cultivated, the internships had, the connections made will spill over into your career no matter where you take it. That being said, I live in Los Angeles and made the east coast move after over 5 years in NYC.

The move from east coast to west coast is one that I did not take lightly, I was moving away from the fashion epicenter to the entertainment capital of the USA and I knew it was risky.

Los Angeles, like other major cities (Miami, Chicago, etc.), has quite a bourgeoning creative scene outside of entertainment. And, the best part is...it's accessible and ready to be tapped. Starting my own marketing and events agency, along with my business partner, would seem daunting in NYC but LA supports and fosters small business in a way that NYC can't, strictly due to the price of running businesses there. LA allows you to tap into a different type of fashion community including up and coming designers, the denim world, and more!

My NYC experience, of course, was and is invaluable and I use it on a daily basis; however, both coasts can foster your career in different ways. I recommend looking into the city that best fits not only your career but also your general lifestyle. Find that match and you will find a community that will inspire and foster your career.

Most importantly, create your own path.

– Jaclyn Johnson, Partner, No Subject

Additional Career Move Considerations

Where are your favorite brands or designer's corporate headquarters? For example, Anthropologie, Urban Outfitters and Free People are based out of Philadelphia. Southern California is home to big surf brands like Reef and Quiksilver. ModCloth has an office in San Francisco, and Tom's Shoes is in based in LA.

Grab a pen or think through the following additional considerations to help you narrow down a few different places you might like to live.

- Are you an independent person who likes to do things alone or do you prefer to have a circle of friends around you?
- Do cities excite or overwhelm you?
- Are you a nature girl that needs a lot of green space?
- Are you an impeccably coiffed designer diva or a surfer girl with a love for flattering board shorts?
- Do you get homesick? Can you afford the plane ticket/train/bus ticket home if you are?
- Are you in love with public transportation or does the convenience of driving your groceries home sound more appealing?

Take all this research into your pot and stir until you have a few fashionable cities that meet your criteria. Then, just like when you visited different colleges, plan a visit.

Put your networking skills to use and begin cultivating relationships with friends or professionals in the city of your choice. Ask your existing network for connections and come up with a few specific questions to ask over email or phone to get a feel for the area. These relationships can provide a couch to sleep on for a few weeks, important locals' only-info or even an interview.

While you are there, make time to visit a business of interest to get a feel for the atmosphere—just walk by or try and score an informational interview. Even if you have a few friends in the area, make time to wander around by yourself to get to know the neighborhood one on one. A little retail therapy, an amazing cup of rose tea...you never know what you might find that lets you know this place could be your new home.

Small(er) Town Fashion PR

If you, for whatever reason, decide to stay put right where you are. Here are a few suggestions to help you explore ways to get involved with the local fashion communities is smaller towns and cities

Befriend Local Media

Most cities have at least one lifestyle magazine that showcases good food, shops, community happenings and entertainment. It may not be *Vanity Fair*. but it is the right place to start getting involved at a local level.

Become the Media

Start your own blog that explores your city from a fashion and retail perspective. Not only will you hone in on your media skills, but every boutique interviewed could be a potential client later on.

Work for Free (or Trade)

Offer to do a press kit for your favorite local boutique and then use your skills to land a cover story or throw a great event. You could offer your services gratis, or for a monthly shopping budget!

Give Back

Charity fashion shows happen in every town. Connect with local charitable organizations and offer your assistance. Not only does working to promote and produce a fashion show look great on your resume, the whole experience will put you front and center among local influencers in your community, as well as local businesses including fashion designers, boutiques, make-up artists, models, and sponsors.

JOURNEY

Ask Yourself: What do I want to be known for, to create, affect, or change?

In the same way that you might design a strategic plan for a client, it's important to have a strategic plan in mind for yourself. Of course it's going to change as you (and your circumstances) change, but you've got to start somewhere right? Plus, When the job hunt (or the job) gets tough, it's helpful to remind yourself what it's all for.

In the beginning of your career, you are in an information-gathering phase, not only learning what it takes to be successful but processing a ton of information – protocol, expectations, office politics, client quirks, learning what kind of coffee gets you through the day – it can feel overwhelming if you aren't grounded in a few pre-determined goals. The following exercises will help you to get clear about what it is you want out of your career. You may want to get a special notebook or create a vision or inspiration board where you tack, paste or otherwise keep track of your career path as it unfolds.

Set Career Goals

Every PR plan starts with identifying goals. What is the purpose of the program (goals), what are we setting out to achieve (objectives), what approach we will use to achieve those things (strategies), the steps we need to take (tactics and tasks) and how will we measure success. The same can be said for your career. So, haute mama (or gent!), what do you want to get out of your professional life? How will you know when you have reached your goal (and it's time to make some new ones!).

You can create short-term or long-term goals, or a mix. Imagine how fun it will be 10 years down the road to take a look at your original career goals – and to see how much you have accomplished!

Here are a few examples:

> **Goal:** I want to work closely with fashion designers and feel like I am having a direct impact on their ability to feel successful.
> **Action:** I will send an email to the local fashion college and see if there are any opportunities to collaborate with student designers to create press kits.

> **Goal:** I want to find a mentor who inspires me to be creative and confident in all areas of my life.
> **Action:** I will attend at least one fashion or business related networking event each month.

> **Goal:** I want to travel three months out of the year for my job
> **Action:** I will apply to PR agencies with international offices.

Set Job Goals

Depending on the agency or brand you work for, you may have to create quarterly or annual goals. Even if this isn't part of the professional development process where you work, make sure to create short-term goals for yourself that are specific to your current place of employment. Try to create goals that are realistic and achievable. Professional goals work best when they are measurable.

Here are a few to get you started:

Goal: This year I will secure three clients editorial placement in *Vogue.*

Action: I will read *Vogue* every month and keep a list of which editors write what types of stories and begin sending emails at least every two weeks sharing something of value with each editor.

Goal: Within three years of beginning my professional career, I am making $50,000 a year.

Action: I will make sure to hold my employers accountable for performance reviews. I will take any recommendations for improvement to heart and develop a plan to achieve them.

Goal: I want to be seen as a fashion PR expert.

Action: I will meet secure at least one speaking engagement each quarter where I demonstrate my knowledge to my local community.

Create a Vision

When things are going well, life has a tendency to fly by. As you apply for jobs, interview, find yourself reading fashion blogs until 2 am, take classes in strange subjects, fall in love, travel, discover that you love sweet potatoes and mid-century furniture but hate spin class etc., it can be easy to forget that you are in fact, living your life right now. There is nothing to wait for, nothing that begins once you land that perfect job, get the promotion, or land a killer front-page story. Before you get drawn in, I encourage you to take some time to think critically about what you really want out of your life. One of the ways to do this is to create a vision board, book or blog, to daydream (really!) and to take tiny actions each day that move you toward your goals.

To kick off the watch-out-world, here comes super-aware, super-powered you, try the following exercise. Find a quiet place where you won't be distracted and give yourself about 15-20 minutes.

Tip: You may want to have a friend read the prompt to you, or record yourself reading it aloud first.

Imagine a perfect day. You wake up, where are you? What kinds of linens are on the bed? Look out the window, what do you see? Head to the kitchen to make breakfast, how do you feel? What are you getting ready to do? Where are you headed? Imagine yourself going through your day. Where do you work? Do you work for someone? Do you work for yourself? What tasks are you working on? How do you feel? What are you wearing? What are you having for lunch? What does your desk look like? How is it decorated? How do you feel?

If you like, write this down in a notebook or in a document. You can even title it, "My Perfect Day." Make sure to write everything in the present tense, and have fun! Here's an example to get you started:

I am the owner of a successful fashion PR firm with offices in New York and Milan. I just got back from fashion week in Paris and I have yet to unpack my luggage. I'm so glad they sent over the new Prada luggage, that black leather trunk was a godsend! I've just finished the most delicious soy cappuccino and I'm waiting for my assistant Molly to arrive. She is going to unpack me while Ernesto does my hair and make-up for the gala tonight. I leave for Turkey in two days, Erin (Fetherston), and I been planning this trip for ages!

And so on. Sounds pretty good, right?

FINAL THOUGHTS

You are already amazing.

Life isn't always an *Ugly Betty* or *Devil Wears Prada* step away from a big break, but persistence and passion does pay off. It can be hard to stay positive while you are in the process of starting your career, so treat your job hunt like a career. Get up, take a shower and get dressed. Spend the morning sending out resumes, the afternoon networking on Twitter by participating in a PR chat, and the evenings knowing you did all you could do, relaxing and having some fun!

While you wait for the request for interviews to come pouring in, explore volunteer opportunities or hobbies. There's nothing better than doing something good for someone else when you're feeling blue. Not only will this do-good attitude build you up, but it also reflects well on your character when you can tell a future employer that instead of sitting at home watching old episodes of Gossip Girl, you trained for a half-marathon, cuddled kittens at the Humane Society or provided after-school tutoring to at-risk kids. Finally, when times get hard, turn to mentors and friends to help you remember your dreams and how far you have already come.

Additionally, I find it helpful to remember that we are not our jobs. It can be easy to allow professional success, or lack thereof, to define our worth. This is simply not the case. While it is important to bring your best self to work, to do your best work and to find work that you enjoy, never allow your job to define your value or let job difficulties or employment fears to keep you stuck in situations that aren't healthy. When times are rough, know that it is your attitude, choices and persistence that will ultimately steer you where you want to be.

Here's one final exercise to help you on your path.

Take a notebook and make three columns. In the first, write down the qualities you admire most in yourself. Then, ask a few friends, a mentor, and your favorite teacher, to each tell you three qualities they like best about you. Stick those in the second column. In the third, write down a few aspirational qualities, things you would like people to recognize about you 3-5 years from now.

Then, take all those qualities, and stick them in a Wordle (Google it!). Play around until you get it looking just right, and then print it out and frame it.

Look at it every day.

GLOSSARY

Every industry has its own vocabulary, a shorthand, if you will, for communication. Ensure you're speaking the language by knowing the definitions of the following terms:

Boilerplate: In PR, the boilerplate refers to a short paragraph of text that communicates key information and attributes about a company or brand. The boilerplate is used in several places, most notably at the end of a press release.

About PR Couture
PR Couture is an online resource covering public relations, marketing and social media for the fashion industry. Created by fashion marketing expert Crosby Noricks in 2006, the site was named one of 25 Essential PR Blogs by PR Web and includes a job board and thriving social media presence. Visit prcouture.com for more information

Calendar listing: Most publications, television stations and local news websites have a place to submit events to be included in an upcoming events section. These are known as calendar listings.

"I've spent the entire morning posting next month's Charity Fashion Show to our local media calendar listings."

Clip: Each time a client is included in a story, photo spread, interview etc, the article is "clipped" and put in a clip book. This can be the physical copies of articles, or in digital form.

"It's only my first day but I've already updated all the clip books for the past three months of coverage."

Copy: the text included in a press release, email pitch, brochure, or website (sometimes called web copy).

"Can you proofread the copy in this media alert?"

Credit: When an item has been chosen for inclusion in a magazine, someone from the credit department will often call the fashion PR agency or designer directly to do a credit check. This ensures that the garment in question is properly named in the magazine and that purchase information is correct.

"Nice! We just got a credit check for the green wool jacket from Lucky Magazine for their November issue."

Desk side: A desk-side is when a fashion PR schedules a short meeting, typically around 15 minutes, to introduce a client to an editor. These often take place at the editor's desk, hence the name.

"Can't wait for today's desk side with the beauty editor at Allure."

Editorial calendar: Most major magazines (and some blogs) create editorial calendars for prospective advertisers that outline the major stories and themes for the next year. PR uses "ed-cals" to link pitches with stories or themes the magazine has planned, like sending over information about an eco-friendly designer for an upcoming green issue.

"According to the ed-cal, Seventeen is focusing on travel in May, we should pitch the new travel bags for consideration."

Fact sheet: Often included as part of a press or media kit, a fact sheet provides media information about a brand that can be read quickly.

"Let me send over the fact sheet, it should have everything you need for your story."

Front-of-house: When hosting a fashion show, many fashion brands will use two different agencies to help manage press, production and flow. Invitations, seating charts and press management is handled by "the front of house," while the actual production of the show is managed by "the back of house."

"Check with Prima Donna PR about your invitation, sweetie, they're running front-of-house."

Glossies: Glossies are monthly fashion magazines, often used to refer to the big guns like Vogue, W, etc. These are also referred to as monthlies or long-lead pubs (short for publications).

"It's nice that we've gotten all this blog coverage, but what we really need is a hit in one of the glossies."

Gift guide: Gift guides are recurring features that fashion editor's put together around a specific season or event. The most well known of these is the holiday gift guide.

"I know it's only May, but we need to start thinking about holiday gift guides."

Gifting suite: Gifting suites often take place before a celebrity award show and include multiple brands eager to converse and push product on celebrities.

"Make sure to take pictures of all the celebs when they come by our booth at the Oscar's gifting suite."

Lead time: The amount of time a publication needs in order to consider your client or story for an upcoming issue. Traditionally, glossies have a three-month lead time.

"The editor wrote back and said they would need at least a 2 month lead time but to try again next season."

Lookbook: Each season, many designers release a lookbook featuring clothing from their latest collection. Sometimes the looks are styled, like a photo shoot, while other times the lookbook is a series of photographs showcasing each garment shot against a white background (this makes it easy for media to include photos in upcoming stories).

"Please review the attached lookbook for consideration."

Op-ed: An op-ed refers to a personal opinion-style article written by somebody other than the journalistic staff. Oftentimes public relations practitioners will pitch clients to write op-eds in the local newspaper.

"The op-ed about eco-friendly fabrics will be included in Sunday's Seattle Times."

Media list: Refers to a list of media names and contact information used for PR outreach.

"Half of the people on this media list no longer work where it says they work."

Media coverage: Also known as editorial coverage or getting "a hit", this refers to any type of press received on behalf of a client, most often the result of PR outreach.

"My favorite part of PR is securing media coverage."

Samples: Designers often have a limited-number of samples available that are sent out to magazines and the like to be reviewed, photographed and/or used in a photo shoot.

"Can you send me the tracking number for the samples we sent to Elle this morning?"

Pitching: Pitching is the process fashion PR's use to communicate client information to an editor. Pitching can take place over the phone, in person or via email and sometimes even over Twitter or Facebook.

"I've sent out 10 pitches this morning, it's time for a triple cappuccino."

Tracking sheet: Sometimes included as part of a media list, the tracking sheet notes when initial pitches, follow-up, pending and secured media coverage occurs.

"According to the tracking sheet, the Daily Candy email should go out next Thursday."

The trades: Trade press refers to business-to-business (B2B) publications like Women's Wear Daily, as opposed to consumer pubs like US Weekly.

"Let's brainstorm story ideas for the trades."

Weeklies: Refers to publications that publish on a weekly basis, also known as short-leads.

"I love pitching the weeklies, you don't have to wait months to see your client in print!"

READING LIST

Books

Groundswell, Expanded and Revised Edition: Winning in a World Transformed by Social Technologies by Charline Li

Fashion 2.0: Blogging Your Way to The Front Row by Yuli Ziv

Fashion Brands: Branding Style from Armani to Zara by Mark Tungate

Fashion Public Relations by Gerald Sherman

If You Have to Cry, Go Outside: And Other Things Your Mother Never Told You by Kelli Cutrone

In Fashion: From Runway to Retail, Everything You Need to Know to Break Into the Fashion Industry by AnneMarie Iverson

Luxury Fashion Branding: Trends, Tactics, Techniques by Uche Okonkwo

Start Something That Matters by Blake Mycoskie

The Pocket Guide to Fashion PR by Sophie Sheikh

The Pocket Guide to Fashion Media by Sophie Sheikh

The Mesh: Why the Future of Business Is Sharing by Lisa Gansky

Will Work For Shoes: The Business Behind Red Carpet Product Placement by Susan Ashbrook

Print/Online

Apparel Insiders

Business of Fashion

California Apparel News

The Cut

DKNY

Fashionably Marketing

Fashion Incubator

Fashionista

Fashion Week Daily

The High Low

Lindsay Olsen

NYC PR Girls

NY Times Fashion

PR Closet

PR Couture

PR Daily

PR Newser

Racked

Retail Minded

Women's Wear Daily (WWD)

WORKS CITED

Cohen, Heidi. "31 Public Relations Definitions." *Heidi Cohen,* March 8, 2011

Ewalt, David M. "Steve Jobs' 2005 Stanford Commencement Address." *Forbes,* October 5, 2011

Tiku, Natasha. "Kelly Cutrone's Advice for PR Succcess." *Inc.,* March 29, 2010

Moreland, Brooke. "Fashion 101: So, What do Fashion Publicists Do." *The Gloss,* March 31, 2010

Reppler, "Managing your online image across social networks." *The Reppler Effect.* September 27, 2011

THANK YOU

This book could not have been completed without the help, contributions and support of the following:

Alyssa Ahern, Anne Buehner, Anne Cecil, Bonny Park, Brianna Saperstein, Brianne Kimmel, Candace Newberry, Carter Boardman, Chris Detert, Connie Wong, Danielle Gano, Dora Maddux, Jaclyn Johnson, Janna Meyrowitz-Turner, Jen Cullen Wilson, Jennifer Bambrough, Jennifer Lezan, Jessica deGuardiola, Jessica Oakes, Kalinda Panzholer, Katie Drain, Kristen Steinhilber Calavas, Laura Perez, Lauren Applebaum, Lauren Rich, Lee Odden, Leah Jacobson, Lindsay Bailey, Lindsay Garvey, Lindsey Green, Liz Anthony, Maggie Philbin, Melanie Bender, Melissa Davis, Michael Shane Stephens, Nancy Vaughn, Nicole McClellan, Rachel Kay, Rachel Meiss, Red Door Interactive, Rob Hopkins, Sarah Essary, Sasha H. Muradali, Shannon Estrada, Shonte Shannon

In memory of my mom, Judy Harrod. Miss you always.

About the Author

Crosby Noricks has nearly a decade worth of experience in fashion PR and consumer marketing. In 2006, she launched PR Couture, an online resource that explores the role of public relations, marketing and social media in the fashion industry. In 2010 Crosby won "Blogger of the Year" at the InfluenceSD Awards. She has been invited by Microsoft to attend Mercedes-Benz Fashion Week, by *Teen Vogue* and WWDMagic as part of the *Teen Vogue* Blogger Lounge at the WWDMagic Tradeshow, and the inaugural Women in PR Summit in honor of her contributions to the industry.

Crosby is Director of Social Media at Red Door Interactive. She holds a master's degree in Mass Communication and Media Studies from San Diego State University and a B.A. from Pitzer College in Media Studies & Gender/ Feminist Studies.

Lightning Source UK Ltd.
Milton Keynes UK
UKOW032155121212

203591UK00008B/396/P